DATE DUE

Zora Neale Hurston

Writer and Storyteller

Patricia and Fredrick McKissack

Series Consultant: Dr. Russell L. Adams, Chairman,
Afro-American Studies, Howard University

Illustrations by Michael Bryant

❖ *Great African Americans Series* ❖

ENSLOW PUBLISHERS, INC.

Bloy St. & Ramsey Ave.
Box 777
Hillside, NJ 07205
U.S.A.

P.O. Box 38
Aldershot
Hants GU12 6BP
U.K.

To Neysa, Martha, Carol, Joyce, and Ellen: WOW!

Library of Congress Cataloging-in-Publication Data

McKissack, Pat, 1944–
    Zora Neale Hurston, writer & storyteller / Patricia and Fredrick
McKissack.
        p. cm. — (Great African Americans series)
    Includes index.
    Summary: Traces the life of the Harlem Renaissance writer and
folklorist, who worked to preserve the rich storytelling tradition
of African Americans of the South.
    ISBN 0-89490-316-0
    1. Hurston, Zora Neale—Biography—Juvenile literature. 2. Afro-
American novelists—20th century—Biography—Juvenile literature.
3. Folklorists—United States—Biography—Juvenile literature.
[1. Hurston, Zora Neale. 2. Authors, American. 3. Afro-Americans—
Biography.] I. McKissack, Fredrick. II. Title. III. Title: Zora
Neale Hurston, writer and storyteller. IV. Series: McKissack, Pat
1944– Great African Americans series.
PS3515.U789Z784   1992
813'.52—dc20
[B]   92-2588
                                                               CIP
                                                               AC

Printed in the United States of America

10 9 8 7 6 5 4 3 2

Photo Credits: Mr. Stetson Kennedy, Jacksonville, Florida, Prints from Rare Books and
Manuscripts, University of Florida Libraries, pp. 12, 14, 24, 25; Library of Congress, pp. 4,
20, 22; Rare Books and Manuscripts, University of Florida Libraries, pp. 8, 27, 29; Courtesy
of the Carl Van Vechten Estate, Joseph Solomon Executor, Print from Rare Books and
Manuscripts, University of Florida Libraries, p. 21.

Illustration Credit: Michael Bryant

Cover Illustration Credit: Ned O.

Contents

Zora Neale Hurston
Born: January 7, 1891, Eatonville, Florida.
Died: January 28, 1960, Fort Pierce, Florida.

1

Jump at the Sun

Zora was born in 1891 about five miles from Orlando, Florida, in a small town named Eatonville. It was an all-black town founded in 1886.

Zora's father, John Hurston, was a preacher. She and her father didn't get along well. He often spanked Zora for being "sassy."

But her mother, Lucy Hurston, made Zora her special child. Lucy told her daughter to "jump at the sun." Zora grew

up jumping, running, and playing in the Florida sunshine. Zora was tough. She knew how to fight, so the boys let her play with them. But the young girl also loved learning about things. She would slip under the porch to read. Her mother made sure Zora had plenty to read.

Zora always liked going to Joe Clarke's store in Eatonville. Men and women sat on the porch and told stories. Zora enjoyed the stories her neighbors told about tricky rabbits and strong black men. They called these stories "big 'ol lies."

When Zora was thirteen years old, her mother died. Her father married again right away. Zora didn't like her stepmother.

Zora didn't get along with her stepmother, so she left home.

And she still did not get along with her father.

Soon Zora was old enough to understand her mother's words. It was time to "jump at the sun!" She couldn't really jump high enough to touch the sun. But if she tried, at least she would be up off the ground! As soon as she could, Zora left home.

2

On the Road

Zora joined a traveling show company. She took care of the costumes. She spent long hours mending and sewing, packing and unpacking. It was hard work. But at least she was away from the father and stepmother she didn't like. Zora felt lucky that she was getting to see some of the world.

Still, she never gave up the idea of going back to school. In 1917 Zora left the show company. She went to a high school

Zora (center) with classmates at Howard University in Washington, D.C. Zora belonged to a writers' group there. She published her first stories in the group's magazine which was called *The Stylus*.

in Baltimore, Maryland. She had one dress, one pair of shoes, and no money. She graduated from high school in June 1918.

Then she went to college in Washington, D.C., for two years. During that time, Zora began writing. She was asked to join a writers' group at the college. Zora wrote her first short story, "John Redding Goes to Sea." It was printed in the writers' group magazine, *The Stylus*, in May 1921. Zora knew then that she could be a writer.

Zora's writing was different from other writers at that time. She wrote about southern blacks and used the language she heard them speak.

3

Making It in New York

In the 1920s many African Americans were leaving the South and moving to northern cities. Many of them moved to New York City. Zora went there in 1925.

She settled in Harlem, a mostly black neighborhood in New York City. In the 1920s, many African American writers, artists, and musicians lived and worked there. Their work was fresh and different. This famous period of time was called the

Harlem Renaissance. Zora Neale Hurston
was one of those fresh young writers.

A lot of white people were interested in
Harlem. Many of them wanted to help the
young writers, too. They met the writers
and poets at parties and helped them get
their work into magazines and books.
These people were called patrons.

One person who helped Zora was Mrs. Charlotte Osgood Mason. She was a very, very rich woman who was a patron to Zora and several other writers and artists.

Zora entered a writing contest. Two of her short stories won. So, she was invited to the awards dinner. Fannie Hurst, a white writer, was a judge in the contest. She liked Zora's work very much. They met at

the awards dinner. Hurst learned that Zora needed a job so she could go back to school. She hired Zora to be her secretary.

At last Zora had enough money to go back to college. Up until that time she had worked two or three jobs at a time to make ends meet.

Hurst also helped Zora get into Barnard College, a women's college at Columbia University in New York City. Zora was the only black woman in Barnard at the time.

During that time Zora still wrote stories. And her writing was getting stronger and better. She graduated from Barnard in 1928.

4

The Voice of Her People

Zora was very interested in studying the ways different people lived. She listened to their stories and folklore. With the help of her patrons, Zora traveled all over the South gathering African American stories. Her research was like sitting on Joe Clarke's store porch listening to people tell stories all the time. She loved it!

Zora was one of the first African Americans to write these stories down. These were the stories of her people, and

In 1927, Zora was given a grant from the Negro Historical Society. She studied the last boatload of slaves who were brought to the United States.

she recorded them in the language of her people. She would write about a storm like this: "God was grumbling his thunder and playing the zigzag lighting thru his fingers."

Her book *Mules and Men* was a collection of her stories and it was written in 1935. Zora was well known for her short stories. In the 1930s she also wrote three novels. The most famous of them was *Their Eyes Were Watching God*, written in 1937. She also wrote her life story, *Dust Tracks on a Road*, in 1942.

Zora also wrote scripts for a radio station in Ohio.

Zora was well liked. She was also a happy person who was always the life of the party. She was known for being a wonderful storyteller.

5

A Very Special Writer

People enjoyed being around Zora. She charmed them with stories about her life in Eatonville. Sometimes her stories were true. Sometimes they weren't. Very few people ever knew the difference.

Zora was married twice, but not for long. She didn't talk about that much. Her first love was writing and her second was her freedom.

Zora continued to study and write about folklore during the 1930s and 1940s. She

During her travels, Zora talked to people on buses, trains, in restaurants, in stores, and even on the street. She believed every person had a story to tell and she was always willing to listen.

traveled through the South, and to Central America, South America, Haiti, and Jamaica. There, she gathered the stories people told.

In 1948 Zora was falsely accused of hurting a child. She was arrested, but they were mistaken. She had been in Central America at the time of the crime. The charges were dropped, but she was very upset.

Zora (front) traveled to the British West Indies and South America looking for stories. Sometimes her travels took her to places she had read about when she was a girl in Eatonville.

By now, all the parties were over. All the friends had gone. Zora chose to live alone in the South, away from friends and family. But she didn't feel sorry for herself.

Zora didn't write much in her last years except for a few articles and short stories. Her books didn't make a lot of money. When she ran out of money, she would take a job as a maid.

Zora wrote many books in her lifetime, but she didn't make a lot of money. Many times she couldn't pay her bills. To earn money, Zora taught at a university and worked as a maid. The only work she ever enjoyed and thought was important was writing.

She moved back to New York in 1957 in order to work on a book. The book was never finished. Zora moved back to Florida and died a poor woman on January 28, 1960. She was buried in an unmarked grave.

Zora Neale Hurston might have been forgotten if it hadn't been for Alice Walker, another black writer. She worked hard to have Zora's old stories turned into books again. Walker had a headstone put on Zora's grave in 1973.

Zora wrote the stories people told her. They were a lot like the stories she heard when she was growing up. If she hadn't gathered them, those stories might have been lost forever.

Today Zora Neale Hurston's books are being read and enjoyed by people all over the world. She was one of the first black woman novelists and folklorists.

Words to Know

folklore—The stories of a group of people that were not written down, but are passed by word of mouth from one generation to another.

graduate—To finish the required studies at a school.

Harlem—A mostly black neighborhood in New York City.

Harlem Renaissance—During the 1920s young black writers, artists, and musicians began showing the black experience in a bold new way. They were not ashamed of being black. They spoke about being proud, beautiful people. *Renaissance* means "an awakening" or "rebirth."

novels—Fictional stories that usually have over 50,000 words in them.

patron—A very rich person who helps a person's work in the arts by giving them money and other help. Zora was able to go to school, travel, and write because she had several patrons.

research—To gather information for study or for discovery. Zora researched stories of the African Americans.

secretary—A person who manages the day-to-day work of an office, or assists a person in their work. Fannie Hurst hired Zora as her secretary.

short stories—Short pieces of fiction, usually found in newspapers and magazines.

traveling show company—A group of performers who travel from place to place, putting on shows.

Index